MEDIUMSHIP
MADE EASY

A Guide to Connect with Your Intuitive Self

Phyllis Okon

Copyright © 2023 by Phyllis Okon

All rights reserved.

Paperback. ISBN: 978-1-950080-11-3

No part of this publication may be reproduced, stored in a retrieval system, or transmitted in any form or by any means, electronic, mechanical, photocopying, recording, scanning, or otherwise, without the prior written permission of the author.

Limit of Liability/Disclaimer of Warranty: This publication is designed to provide accurate and authoritative information in regard to the subject matter covered. It is sold with the understanding that neither the author nor the publisher is engaged in rendering legal, investment, accounting or other professional services. While the publisher and author have used their best efforts in preparing this book, they make no representations or warranties with respect to the accuracy or completeness of the contents of this book and specifically disclaim any implied warranties of merchantability or fitness for a particular purpose. No warranty may be created or extended by sales representatives or written sales materials. The advice and strategies contained herein may not be suitable for your situation. You should consult with a professional when appropriate. Neither the publisher nor the author shall be liable for any loss of profit or any other commercial damages, including but not limited to special, incidental, consequential, personal, or other damages.

For Tracey Soussi- Thanks for sharing this journey.

Special thanks to my sons, Michael and Eric, who keep me on my toes and have made sure I am the "mother of reinvention."

CONTENTS

Introduction | 1
Chapter 1 | 3
Chapter 2 | 9
Chapter 3 | 11
Chapter 4 | 13
Chapter 5 | 15
Chapter 6 | 19
Chapter 7 | 27
Chapter 8 | 35
Chapter 9 | 41
Chapter 10 | 43
Reading Material | 45
About the Author | 57

INTRODUCTION

MEDIUMS CAN CONNECT the living world with spirits on the other side.

Some people are born with this ability. They discover early that they can see, hear, or feel things that most others cannot. It comes to them naturally, without effort. Until they learn exactly what these powers are, they can be confused, angry, and isolated. These gifts can make them feel different, and they are forced to learn how to control the information to have a productive existence. Many are forced to keep their capabilities to themselves for fear of ridicule.

Only recently, mediumship has been brought out of the shadows and discussed respectfully. However, there is still a huge population still treats mediumship with disbelief, terror, and fear.

Some believe that mediumship is a gift given only to a select group. Others think it can be inherited through family DNA. However, mediumship is a practice that anybody can master.

By understanding and exercising a few disciplines, anybody can learn to raise their vibration, cut out the everyday noise, and learn to hear the messages constantly streaming inside their heads.

Whether you want to learn so that you can communicate with a loved one, turn this into a new revenue stream, or just out of curiosity, enjoy the journey. You may gain a deeper understanding of yourself and the world around you.

CHAPTER 1

What is a medium?

A MEDIUM IS A person who can connect with loved ones on the other side and communicate with them.

Mediums can use different tools or plug into the universe. They include channeling, dowsing rods, crystals, ouija boards, tarot, seances, trances, and physical mediumship.

Mediumship or spiritualism arrived in the mainstream during the nineteenth century when it became a new and fun source of entertainment. Mediumship became all the rage, and along with some very gifted people, charlatans interested in exploiting people's grief destroyed genuine practitioners' credibility.

People had mediumship parties with celebrity mediums. However, as time passed and investigations occurred, several spiritualists were exposed as con artists and frauds. Their staged dramatic performances that included lights flickering and tables levitating turned mediumship into a joke. Mediumship was relegated to carnival shows until the late twentieth century, when television mediums rose in popularity, bringing it back in vogue.

Today, several respected mediums share their skills with the police for missing persons and the armed forces for remote viewing.

What are the different types of mediums?

Mental mediums relay messages they see, hear or feel. They use assorted 'clairs,' like clairvoyance or clairaudience, to receive images or sounds, then relay the information to a sitter.

Mediums rarely make predictions. They usually don't discuss career decisions or love life issues. Mediums give messages of healing, comfort, and closure. They open a curtain revealing life is not over when a loved one dies and help in the bereavement process.

Physical mediums are believed to produce materializations or noise while in a seance. A medium might go into a trance, and the spirit uses its body to convey a message. Some physical mediums are tied down because their movements may seem uncontrolled. Their voices change, sounding otherworldly.

Most people are sophisticated enough and need solid proof making evidential mediums the best source for answers.

What is an evidential medium?

An evidential medium provides verifiable information proving they communicate with the spirit world. As stated earlier, some people are born with this ability; others can learn by taking courses.

Evidential mediums prefer not to see or hear anything that might interfere with their information. A good evidential medium will relate information that only the sitter could know.

What is channeling?

Channelers receive messages from their higher selves or the spirit world to relay a message. Trance channeling allows an entity to enter its body as a vehicle to communicate. There is often a special name for the entity or entities they channel.

What is a spirit guide?

A spirit guide is a nonphysical being assigned to help people reach their greatest earthly potential.

Spirit guides have been around since the beginning of time. Everyone has a spirit guide or many guides. They are assigned at birth and accompany the person until the end of their life.

Spirit guides can take many different forms. Vibrating at a higher frequency, they can show up as animals, voices, and visions.

Spirit guides are responsible for bringing soulmates together. They send those thoughts of doubt and apprehension via your gut instinct when a situation is dangerous.

Spirit guides can be an ancestor, a light being, or even your higher self. Spirit guides also show up as angels, archangels, and ascended masters. They can be plant or animal spirits, as well.

Different spiritual traditions describe the angelic realms in various ways. There seems to be agreement that there is a hierarchy of angels, and these groupings are organized by function — like guardian angels, for example. Like spirit guides, angels are also available for direction and protection, and they embody unconditional love, compassion, and wisdom. It is not believed, however, that angels have ever been incarnated in any other form.

How Can I Communicate With Angels?

Angels are ready to hear you anytime you choose. They are not to be worshipped.

Angels, especially guardian angels, are there to keep us safe in harmful situations and work through our intuition or gut to guide us away from dangerous choices.

What Are Archangels?

There are several archangels — such as Michael, Gabriel, and Raphael—and they take care of different areas of our lives. Archangel Michael is the angel most called upon for protection and guidance; Raphael is called in more frequently for health issues. Gabriel is associated with visions and messages, and Uriel is considered the angel of prophecy and wisdom.

What's The Main Difference Between Spirit Guides And Angels?

Spirit guides are more personal and have different energies. Everybody has at least, one whether they recognize them or not. They are assigned at birth.

Angels appear as light beings and don't belong to a person in particular but to everybody. They are there to help.

With training, both spirit guides and angels are accessible.

Are Angels different than spirit guides?

Angels are beings that have never incarnated and lived as a human. They have always lived in the spiritual realm.

Spirit guides have been communicating with you for your entire life through dreams, symbols, and signs. Synchronicities are the work of spirit guides. In other words, nothing is random in our world. Their job is to connect you to your soul's purpose and lean into you during tough times.

Do you keep seeing random collections of numbers or a song on the radio that 'speaks' to your feelings? They might be messages from your spirit guide. Think of them as your lifelong spirit coach.

You can communicate with your spirit guide by simply asking for help. They won't intervene unless you request it.

To connect, you have to acknowledge that they are genuinely there. Start looking for synchronicities and patterns that keep showing up. Understand they are being put there for a reason.

We've discussed spirit guides, ancestors, angels, and archangels; what about our higher selves?

Our higher selves are that part of you that is not attached to our ego or worldly body. It's a non-material version of yourself that is part of the universal consciousness. Some consider it their soul or spirit.

In many religions, when a person connects with the Divine, it is said that they are connecting with their higher self.

CHAPTER 2

What is the difference between mediumship and psychic abilities?

THERE IS A big difference between psychics and mediums. People often confuse the two. The contrast is starkly apparent in the reading the person desires.

Psychics use intuition to tap into the universe and receive information regarding a person's past, present, or future. By connecting with the sitter's higher self or spirit guide, they can share specific knowledge about someone they could not have known.

A psychic is useful to help you decide about your future or give you some insight to help point you in the right direction. They include information about your relationships, career, finances, and health.

Mediums connect with a sitter's loved ones on the other side. An evidential medium provides specific data proving they communicate with your loved one. They can also communicate with pets, miscarriages, and ancestors.

Mediums rarely make predictions. They usually don't discuss career decisions or love life issues.

Mediums give messages of healing, comfort, and closure. They open a curtain revealing life is not over when a loved one dies and help in the bereavement process.

Both psychics and mediums can use tools to help them connect. Runes, tarot cards, pendulums, crystals, automatic writing, and dowsing rods are some of the different things employed to determine this knowledge.

Most mediums are psychic, but a psychic is rarely a medium.

In short, if a sitter is looking to find out if they should change jobs or leave a toxic situation, they should seek a psychic.

If they desire a message from a loved one that has passed, then they need a medium.

CHAPTER 3

Where is my third eye, and what does it do?

The third eye is located between the eyebrows. It is associated with a chakra found in that area. Chakras are believed to be wheel-like energy centers throughout our bodies. When they are out of balance, we are off-center.

The third-eye chakra is called Ajna and is linked to perception, awareness, spiritual communication, and inner wisdom. It connects us to visualizations and the truth. It opens the gateway to clairvoyance and taps into our psychic abilities.

This particular chakra is linked to the pineal gland, a pea-sized gland shaped like a pine cone near the brain's pituitary gland. It is said to be the organ of supreme universal connection and is considered important in cultures throughout the world.

Cultivating your third eye is the gateway to becoming a psychic or medium. When it is blocked, some symptoms are uncertainty, confusion, headaches, depression, pessimism, lack of direction, and cynicism. Many things can interfere with your third eye. They include an unbalanced diet, too much processed food, a disconnect with nature, and metal exposure.

While your eyes see the world, the third eye sees the true world.

Some say that surrounding yourself with crystals it might activate the third eye.

The third eye is associated with amethyst, sodalite, purple sapphire, and purple tourmaline.

The practice of yoga helps to open the third eye, as well as repeating positive affirmations.

CHAPTER 4

What is automatic writing, and what will it do for me?

AUTOMATIC OR SPIRITUAL writing is an exercise in psychic or mediumship ability. Many people feel that spirit guides and our higher self message us through our hands.

Automatic writing is a way to channel subconscious thoughts or get direct messages from other entities. Automatic writing is also known as psychography because both mediums and psychics claim they produce messages without consciously writing. They are being manipulated by something other than this world.

Automatic writing is as simple as getting a clean piece of paper or a pad and a pen and writing whatever comes into your mind. If you prefer using a computer, the concept is the same. Sit at the keyboard and let your fingers fly.

Don't try to think too much while practicing it. Let the pen or fingers be an extension of your thoughts, and don't read what you are writing. Forget about spelling or content.

Transfer the thoughts without judgment or inhibitions.

Many people practice automatic writing before leaving bed in the morning. They keep a journal beside them, and write before they start their day. Dreams are still fresh now as well.

Ask your higher self to give you any messages you need to know.

Take three cleansing breaths, and write whatever comes into your head. Don't think about it. It can be doodles, a message, a letter to yourself… anything.

CHAPTER 5

What is the Monkey Mind?

According to Eastern philosophies, the 'monkey mind' reflects a person with a restless, confused, or unsettled mind. The monkey mind is exactly what it sounds like, and out of control entity.

Between electronics and social media, the monkey mind has taken over. People have shorter attention spans and have a hard time trying to focus.

Picture a mouse on a wheel or stuck in a maze. It's when the mind jumps from subject to subject without any satisfaction of finishing a thought. That wild energy prevents both creativity and spirit in the mind from receiving messages.

Thoughts balloon and are out of control. When you fret or worry, obsession takes over. The monkey mind is addictive, and everybody has this tiny monkey creating havoc in their thoughts.

To proceed, you must shut down that monkey mind and allow thoughts to float by. We must become the observer rather than the participant.

How do we control the monkey mind?

It's as simple as calming the mind, being in the present, or being mindful. This will open your mind and soul, allowing them to connect your inner and outer worlds. Like tuning a radio, it will permit you to accept the messages that have been there all along.

Being mindful is focusing your awareness only on the present. It is a state of affirmation. It's not meditative but an extreme acceptance of living in the moment.

When do you feel disconnected? Think of when you are reflecting on an idea. Your thoughts are passive; they float by without interaction. It happens while driving, listening to music, getting a manicure, or even food shopping. It's when you go through the motions, musing without actively thinking.

You have to go to that place of passive thought and, using breathing techniques, filter your thoughts and let yourself float.

Breathing Exercises

Alternate-nostril breathing is a wonderful technique to help you feel centered.

Begin by inhaling and exhaling through both nostrils. Then, inhale through only the left nostril while closing off the right with your finger. Then repeat with the other side while holding the left nostril shut.

Breathing exercises can help reduce stress and is good for the heart, blood pressure, lungs, and brain.

Identify when your brain is in monkey mind mode, and use either meditation or a breathing exercise, forcing it to slow down. You may sleep better as well.

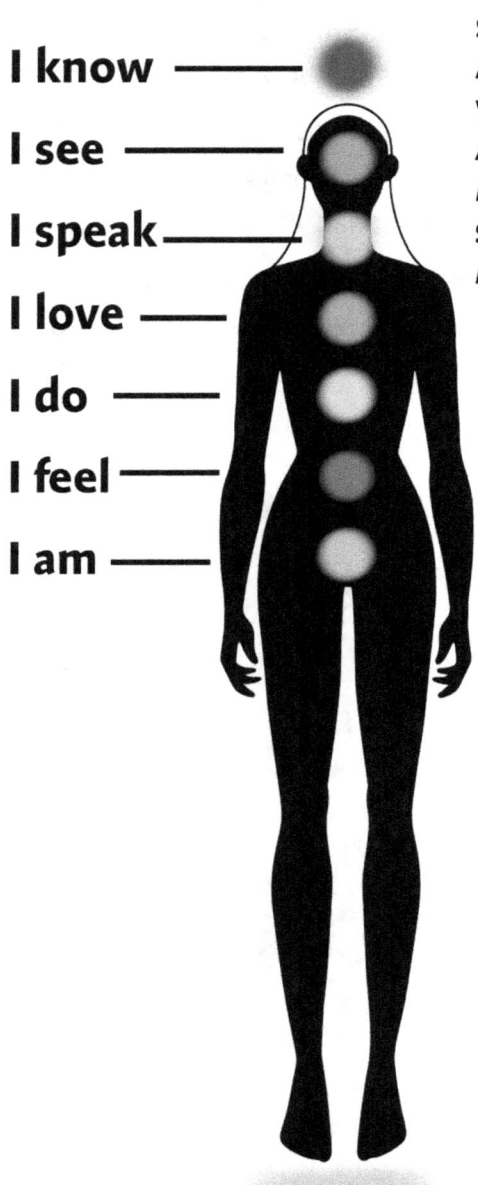

CHAPTER 6

Chakras, Grounding, and Protection

In Sanskrit, the word chakra means wheel. The wheels represent the seven major energy centers in the body, and when they spin in unison, all is well. Each wheel corresponds to an organ and nerve cluster along the body's center.

Chakras need to move together and stay open and balanced. When they become blocked, a person can begin to feel emotional or physical symptoms.

Energy follows intention and is governed by our thoughts and feelings. This triggers our Chakras to transmit energy in different directions, quantities, and rates of speed.

The Chakras act as depots that store and send our energy where it needs to go.

There are over 88,000 Chakras in the body. We will concentrate on the main chakras that run along the spinal column and make up the Human Energy System. It starts with the crown and ends with the root.

Root Chakra

The root chakra, or Muladhara, can be found at the base of the spine. It grounds you to the earth and provides a foundation for life. Rooting to the earth allows you to feel grounded and withstand challenges. Your root chakra is responsible for your sense of stability and security. The color red always represents the root chakra.

Sacral Chakra

The sacral chakra, or Svadhisthana, is just below your navel. This chakra is responsible for your creative and sexual energy. It connects how you relate to your emotions as well as the emotions of others. Orange is the color of the sacral chakra.

Solar Plexus Chakra

The solar plexus chakra, or Manipura, is found in your stomach region. It's responsible for helping you feel in control of your life. It is the place where you get your confidence and self-esteem. This is where the concept of fight or flight comes from. Like the sun, the solar plexus is the color yellow.

Heart Chakra

The heart chakra, or Anahata, is found in the center of your chest near your heart. The heart chakra is green and all about our ability to love and show compassion. It defines how we relate to others.

Throat Chakra

This chakra, or Vishuddha, is in your throat and bright blue. This area has to do with communication. It represents both verbal and nonverbal language. When it is out of balance, you might not feel you have a voice or that people do not hear you.

Third Eye Chakra

The third eye chakra, or Ajna, is between your eyes. This chakra is responsible for intuition and insight. The third eye is linked to our imagination and is purple.

Crown Chakra

The crown chakra, or Sahasrara, is at the top of your head. It represents your spiritual connection to yourself, as well as everything around you. Think of it as a violet or pure white cord connecting you to the universe. It also plays a role in your life's purpose.

What does it mean if a Chakra is unbalanced?

When chakras are blocked or imbalanced, it manifests in various ways.

An overactive chakra will produce energy that interferes with a person's life. If it is low on energy, there might be difficulties expressing the representations of that chakra.

If you are feeling insecure, you might have to work on the root chakra to ground yourself and find your footing. If there is too much energy, it might show up as fearlessness. They must be balanced; too much of anything is not good.

Can a blocked chakra affect your health?

The wobbly chakra may affect the parts of your body near that particular chakra. It could throw anything from organs to bones out of balance and manifest as pain.

Psychologically, an out-of-tune chakra can cause an emotional imbalance leading to depression, fear, and anger.

Too much stress, either physical or mental, can cause one or more chakras to be out of balance.

It's important to eat right, exercise, and treat your body in the best way possible.

Prolonged imbalances could cause physical disease and illness, bone pain, and mental health issues like depression or anxiety.

How can you unblock a chakra?

A great way to promote balance in a chakra is to align your physical body by doing the following

- yoga

- breathing practices like alternate nostril breathing described in the previous chapter,
- meditation

Raising your vibration

These three practices are the foundation of raising your vibration.

Start by slowing your breathing.

Start at the crown and allow the white light to penetrate your skull, then work down your chakras. Imagine spinning wheels in the appropriate color. Bathe that area of your body with that color, and try to get them to sync up with each other. Pay attention to any soreness or feeling out of balance, and spend more time there.

A Reiki master can align chakras and draw out imbalances.

Crystals

People use crystals to balance their chakras. They surround themselves with the one that corresponds to the area needing attention.

Crystals have been used for thousands of years for healing and balancing. Educate yourself on the properties and where they have the most influence, and buy the ones that speak to you.

Sound Baths

Gongs, bowls, and music have played a role in ritual healing since the beginning of time. It is said that sounds can affect our brainwaves, making us more receptive and relaxed. Seek out sounds that make you feel good.

Meditation

Meditation soothes the brain. It helps with anxiety and can bring clarity to thoughts.

Yoga

Yoga is a Hindu discipline of exercises that include breathing control, meditation, and moving into certain poses. People doing yoga train to hold them for as long as they can. Doing this, it makes them go deeper in both mind and body and ultimately raises their vibration.

Grounding

What is grounding, and is it important?

Grounding is an essential practice that keeps you in the present and helps reorient you to a calmer reality. It's a useful skill to use when anxiety overwhelms or the monkey mind takes over.

When you are grounded, you're in a state of mind that enables you to be aware of what is happening in the present moment. Both body and mind are calm enabling you to focus on one thing. Your brain will stop jumping from one thought to the next. It is important to ground yourself before a reading. This will allow thoughts to clarify more easily and protect you from negative people and thoughts.

Think of it as putting on your armor.

How to ground yourself?

Find a comfortable place. You can be sitting or lying down. It doesn't matter. Start at the top of your head and slowly and methodically place imaginative armor on your body. I picture white armor, and like a Marvel superhero, I feel it cover every inch of my body.

I imagine white light shooting from my hands and feet, connecting and rooting me to the earth, keeping me centered and safe.

Very often, I do this for my loved ones. Covering them in the white light of protection keeps them safe from negativity.

Where do self-doubt and fear come from?

Self-doubt and fear are manifested from traumatic experiences that have happened throughout your life, scaring your psyche. They impact self-esteem and can affect all of your chakras.

It's up to you to conquer self-doubt and fear.

Find the origin of your insecurities and understand their lack of power over you.

Concentrate on past achievements. Stop criticizing yourself - think of life as one extensive life lesson. There are no mistakes, only learning experiences.

Surround yourself with supportive people.

Identify your triggers and realize that you control them, not the other way around.

Replace negative, self-defeating talk with positive affirmations. Nothing works better than a good pep talk.

Don't compare yourself with other people.

And most importantly, be honest with yourself.

CHAPTER 7

What are the 'clairs', and how can I identify mine?

CLAIRVOYANCE IS PROBABLY THE most familiar of all the clairs. It means 'clear-seeing' and comes from French.

The brain is constantly downloading images. We are taught from an early age to ignore all the messages we are getting. Too often, it's said that a child has a vivid imagination or they are making things up. Most likely, they are not. They are subtly and steadily being conditioned not to see, hear, or feel things.

If you are clairvoyant, you see flashes of images or even a quick newsreel. These downloads can happen while you are asleep, meditating, or when you're awake. These images appear to the inner eye, inside your head, which makes it easy to pass off as your imagination.

If your eyes are drawn to an object, like a series of numbers, this is another form of clairvoyance.

Clairaudient

Clairaudient is 'clear hearing.' Psychic information is transmitted through the inner ear. Some clairaudients hear a message, but others get alerted when their ears ring, or get hot for no apparent reason.

People don't realize they are clairaudient when they hear a message in a song on the radio. Sounds can be subtle, heard only in your head.

Many mediums say they hear a bell ringing before they receive a message.

Claircognizance

Claircognizance is a clear sense of knowing something without prior knowledge.

Claircognizants have a perception of things. It feels like information is pouring into the top of their heads.

When a claircognizance does a reading, they have an understanding of the information they are sharing.

Did you ever feel that you just knew something was going to happen, and it does? That is claircognizance. Some people refer to it as intuition.

Clairsentience

Clairsentience is a clear sense of feeling.

Similar to claircognizance, it begins with a gut feeling.

Most people have this but never attribute it to the paranormal. It's so common every day that the receiver doesn't recognize these messages.

Misunderstood and taken for granted, this is when the universe, our angels, or relatives talk to us. Whether it's a warning or a signal of something about to happen, clairsentience is something most people can identify with.

Clairsentience manifests both internally and externally. Our bodies sense a higher vibration and react to it. Goosebumps, a hot flash, and scalp tightening is the body's way of acknowledging a higher vibration or spirit nearby.

Internally, it comes as the sick feeling in your gut, or just knowing you have to make a decision the way your body is indicating.

Clairempathy

Clairempathy is a clear sense of feeling other people's emotions.

Clairempaths can feel emotions without being near the other person. It can manifest as an understanding that something is wrong with the subject in question.

Twins and close siblings share this ability to feel each other's pain or know when something is off with the other.

Clairgustance

Clairgustance is a clear sense of taste. A clairgustance can detect information through their tastebuds.

They can identify the taste of a dish without having it nearby.

Sometimes they can taste blood when someone has died in a tragic accident. It could even be a special dish associated with loved on on the other side. They could have either loved or hated it, but a clairgustance can taste the flavor of that dish.

Clairsalience

Clairsalience is a clear sense of smell.

Smoke, cigars, food, and perfume all fall under this Clair.

Sometimes you get a whiff of your late mom's perfume, and there is no way that could happen. That is a perfect example of clairalience.

Clairtangency

Clairtangency is a clear sense of touch.

Psychics or mediums can detect information through touch or their hands.

Some mediums hold a picture or an object in their hands and get a sense of the person who owned it.

Building your intuitive muscles

1. Meditate

Messages from your intuition tend to be quiet, so spending time in silence will help you hear and understand these messages.

2. Start noticing all that you can with your five senses.

Test them out. See if any feel more active than others.

When you do this, it raises your sensitivity to your sixth sense.

3. Pay attention to your dreams.

When the mind is busy, it can override the intuitive side of your brain and the subconscious mind, where intuition is located. When you're asleep, the cognitive mind rests and opens the subconscious mind to send messages to you using dreams.

4. Get creative

Doing creative activities, such as drawing, singing, dancing, scrapbooking, gardening, or automatic writing, quiets the cognitive mind and allows your intuition to speak up.

5. Learn tarot cards

Take a course on tarot or oracle cards. Try to interpret the pictures on the face of the cards before you check what the guidebook says they mean.

6. Test your gut and intuition

If you have feelings about what might happen in your world, write down your hunches, then check them later. Keep a journal. See how often you were right.

7. Think about what you're feeling

Your intuition speaks to you through your body, and the more you cultivate awareness, the more sensitive you become. If you get an uncomfortable physical feeling, pay attention. Where is it hitting you? Do you feel light or heavy? Got a sick feeling in your gut? It could just be the stress, but it could also be your intuition.

8. Change your routine

Get away. Slow down. Go on a retreat or spend a day with nothing planned. When you're too busy, it's hard to be sensitive to the voices of intuition. Try emptying your schedule and see if your intuition pipes up.

9. Spend time in nature

Being in the natural world, away from technology and the cognitive mind's other temptations, can open up the kind of intuition we needed when we as a species lived outdoors and relied upon it to keep us safe from the elements, predators, and other true fear dangers.

10. Try doing a repetitive movement

Run. Dance. Chop celery. Tap dance. These physical actions can calm the thinking mind and open up your intuition.

11. Practice sensing people before you know them.

See what information you can get from observing people and feeling their energy before you talk to them. Write it down and keep notes. Mark how often your hunch was correct.

12. Trust the message.

Don't think that you're crazy when you get an intuitive hunch. The cognitive mind argues with intuition rather than trusting it. You may rationalize yourself out of intuitive knowledge that could change your life for the better.

13- Don't lose faith in every wrong answer.

It's okay to be wrong. Note what you feel when you get it right. Do you have the chills? Does something on your body stand out?

CHAPTER 8

What are some of the tools mediums and psychic use?

Symbols- what do they mean?

Symbols are one of the most useful and easy tools mediums, and psychics use. Early in their studies, a medium will create a kind of symbol dictionary or, really, Pictionary.

This is a bevy of images that spirit will use to communicate with them.

If a medium sees an apple, it may mean New York City, The Big Apple. It could also mean a teacher.

For instance, when I see big, black rubber boots and suspenders, I know I am talking about a fireman.

The symbols are wholly personal and only have meaning to the medium.

Sometimes, spirit will provide an image, not for the medium to interpret but for the sitter. For example, I saw a squirrel and asked what was the significance of the animal. The sitter laughed and said it was her husband's nickname.

Symbols and images flash. They do not stay long in the mind. A medium has to be quick when giving the information.

A good clue in identifying a message with your imagination is the length of the image in your head. If it stays too long, it's your imagination.

A medium must report only what they see or hear. They must not put their spin on it.

In other words, don't build castles in the air and take your client on a flight of fancy from your imagination.

What are Tarot Cards?

Tarot cards were created in the 1400s in Italy. Originally they were used as playing cards. In France in the 1700s, people assigned meaning to each card, and they were used to divine the future.

Each card in the tarot deck represents a different person and or a lesson.

A reader shuffles the cards and then lays them out in a pattern representing past, present, and future. An interpretation of the cards is revealed for the sitter to receive an important message or give direction to future events.

How many cards are in a Tarot deck?

There are 78 cards in a tarot deck. Twenty-two are called the Major Arcana. The remaining fifty-six are called Minor Arcana.

Like playing cards, they are divided into four suites: Wands, Cups, Swords, and Pentacles or coins.

Each suit has fourteen cards, including ten numbered cards and a Page, Knight, Queen, and King.

How do you read Tarot cards?

There are four steps to reading Tarot cards. First, the reader has to think about your question; then, they select a Tarot spread with positions that relate to the question.

Next, the sitter shuffles the cards and lays them out deliberately in a particular design. Finally, the reader interprets the cards based on their intuition.

Pendulum

A pendulum is a weight or crystal suspended from a chain or thread so that it can swing independently.

Pendulums have been used as a divining tool for thousands of years.

A person asks the pendulum to move in one direction, indicating a positive response. They choose another direction to show a negative one.

This identifies the direction the pendulum is using for answers.

Schoolchildren and midwives use it for simple yes and no questions.

Dowsing Rods

Dowsing rods are two bent brass or metal rods that respond to yes and no questions similar to a pendulum.

First, you have to identify which spirit is helping with the movement of the rods.

The reader asks if their spirit guide or specific ancestor is helping with the answers. Once the name is mentioned and the rods cross, they know who is assisting.

Holding the rods in both hands, the reader asks the rods affirmative and negative questions.

Example Question- Grandma, will I be accepting my new job?

Crystals

People attribute all types of powers to crystals. Some believe they can heal illness in the body, mind, and soul.

Many ancient cultures have used crystals for healing. They believed crystals promoted the flow of good energy.

Crystals are minerals that vibrate on the same level as the human body. It is said that we exchange energies with crystals when we work with them.

Crystals are used for many important household objects. They power lasers, watches, televisions, and other vital equipment.

Healing crystals for health

- Clear quartz: a clear crystal considered a healer and believed to support the entire energetic system
- Jasper: a nurturing stone said to provide comfort during times of stress
- Obsidian: believed to help process in letting go
- Amethyst: used for healing and cleansing
- Bloodstone: said to improve circulation

Healing crystals for wealth

- Tiger's eye: said to lessen fear
- Citrine: believed to spark enthusiasm and creativity
- Turquoise: thought to attract good luck
- Sapphire: known as a stone of prosperity
- Jade: another well-known stone for prosperity and luck

Healing crystals for love

- Rose quartz: believed to encourage love and trust
- Moonstone: said to prompt feelings of inner strength and growth
- Ruby: believed to support sexuality and sensuality

CHAPTER 9

What does setting an intention mean?

Simply put, go through whatever ritual you need to get ready. Some people meditate. Others hold an object, ground themselves, or even hold crystals.

The next step is to talk to your higher self about setting an intention. Ask for spirit guide, a higher self, or deceased loved ones to help you with the reading.

Detach yourself from the outcome. Trust your spirit guide or the universe to deliver the information.

Breakdown of a message

There has to be a structure to delivering a message.

First, state an intention.

Then allow information to be received.

Establish who is coming through to the sitter.

Ask spirit for some evidence to help the sitter identify them.

Deliver the message spirit gives to you. Remember, you are not there to put in your opinion. Don't create a fantasy from the message. Say what you see with responsibility to your sitter's feelings. Be aware that words can hurt, so make sure you read the room and act with compassion.

Sounds pretty anti-climatic. It is not. When you see the faces change from hope to joy, the reunion is so sweet; you understand this is not a game but a sacred mission to bring comfort, peace, and love from one world to another.

CHAPTER 10

Setting up a business

If you want to be taken seriously, you must treat mediumship as a business. Welcome to Startup 101.

Get out a pad and pen because there is much to do.

While most mediums rely on word of mouth and repeat clients, social media is a way for people to learn about your skills.

You will need a corporation to protect yourself and collect your fund. A bank account. You'll need to be able to take charges, so you'll need to set up with a credit card company.

Social media pages, Facebook, Instagram, TikTok, and Youtube, are your best friends. Begin by posting daily and building your audience.

Post information and interesting pictures. Never talk about a session; a sitter should remain anonymous, their readings private. Follow other mediums and see what they do.

Start blogging and see if you can be on other mediums or psychic podcasts.

This is branding. The more people who hear of you, the better your chance of getting customers.

Volunteer to give free readings until you can build up a reputation where you can charge.

Be prepared to hear that you have a gift and should give it away for free. Know that people will use guilt and pity to get free readings. Set your price and then stick to it.

Nobody is expected to work for free. To get a reading, the universe dictates there must be an exchange.

Ethics- learning the code and responsibility of mediumship

What is the responsibility of a medium or psychic?

People are grieving, mourning the loss of a loved one. They are searching for answers, closure, and peace.

It is a medium's job to deliver those types of messages.

Unless you're sure of what you are seeing, hearing, or feeling, don't say it.

I hope you enjoyed this introduction to Mediumship.

May you have a long and happy career!

READING MATERIAL

Many of these books are not devoted exclusively to mediumship but should help you along your journey to self-awareness.

72 Angels of Magick: Instant Access to the Angels of Power - Brand, Damon

Abilities (For Beginners (Llewellyn's)) - William W. Hewitt

Angelic Invocations: Angelic Energy Prayers & Empowering Invocations of Supreme Celestial Light and Love to Heal, Purify, and Uplift Your Life On Earth (Celestial Gifts) (Volume 1) - Mylonas, Georgios

Angelic Reiki: The Healing for Our Time', Archangel Metatron - Core, Christine

Angels: Companions in Magick - RavenWolf, Silver

Angels and Archangels: A Magician's Guide - Echols, Damien

Angels and Archangels in Reiki Practice: A practical guide - Suraj, Haripriya

Angel Tarot - McHenry, Travis

A Radical Approach to the Akashic Records: Master Your Life and Raise Your Vibration - Feick, Melissa

Archangels of Magick: Rituals for Prosperity, Healing, Love, Wisdom, Divination and Success - Brand, Damon

Ask George Anderson: What Souls in the Hereafter Can Teach Us About Life - Anderson, George

Believe In Yourself (Hay House Classics) - Dr. Joseph Murphy

Be Rich!: The Science of Getting What You Want - Robert Collier

Be Yourself: The Art of Relaxation - Regardie, Israel

Buddha's Brain: The Practical Neuroscience of Happiness, Love, and Wisdom - Rick Hanson

Choose Them Wisely: Thoughts Become Things! - Mike Dooley

Concentration Exercises - Grabovoi, Grigori

Corpus Hermeticum: The Divine Pymander - Trismegistus, Hermes

Cosmic Consciousness - M.D. Richard Maurice Bucke

Dancing with Dragons: Invoke Their Ageless Wisdom & Power - Conway, D.J.

Everybody's Guide to Natural ESP: Unlocking the Extrasensory Power of Your Mind - Swann, Ingo

Everyday Karma - Carmen Harra

Financial Success: Harnessing the Power of Creative Thought - Wallace D. Wattles

Gabriel: Communicating with the Archangel for Inspiration & Reconciliation (Angels Series, 2) -

Webster, Richard

George Anderson's Lessons from the Light: Extraordinary Messages of Comfort and Hope from the

Other Side - Anderson, George

Happy for No Reason: 7 Steps to Being Happy from the Inside Out - Marci Shimoff

Healing Magick: Words of Power to Heal Yourself and Others - Manning, Rose

Heaven Is Beautiful: How Dying Taught Me That Death Is Just the Beginning - Panagore, Peter Baldwin

Honoring Your Ancestors: A Guide to Ancestral Veneration - Vaudoise, Mallorie

How to Read the Akashic Records: Accessing the Archive of the Soul and Its Journey - Howe, Linda

How to Talk to the Other Side: Learning How To Communicate With Loved Ones, Spirits and Angels

Infinite Possibilities: The Art of Living Your Dreams - Mike Dooley

Infinite Quest: Develop Your Psychic Intuition to Take Charge of Your Life - John Edward

Instant Self-Hypnosis: How to Hypnotize Yourself with Your Eyes Open - Blair, Forbes

Integrative Hypnosis: A Comprehensive Course in Change - Tiers, Melissa

Is There An Afterlife?: A Comprehensive Overview of the Evidence - David Fontana

It Works: The Famous Little Red Book That Makes Your Dreams Come True! - RHJ

Just Ask the Universe: A No-Nonsense Guide to Manifesting your Dreams - Samuels, Michael

Kabbalah, Magic & the Great Work of Self Transformation: A Complete Course - Christopher, Lyam Thomas

Kabbalah: Key to Your Inner Power (Mystical Paths of the World's Religions) - Elizabeth Clare Prophet

Kabbalah for Health and Wellness: Revised and Updated - Stavish, Mark

Karma: The Ancient Science of Cause and Effect - Jeffrey Armstrong

Law of Attraction: The Science of Attracting More of What You Want and Less of What You

Leveraging the Universe and Engaging the Magic - Mike Dooley

Life After Breath: How a Brush with Fatality Gave Me a Glimpse of Immortality - Cooper, Jacob

Living in a Mindful Universe: A Neurosurgeon's Journey into the Heart of Consciousness - Alexander, Eben

Low Magick: It's All In Your Head ... You Just Have No Idea How Big Your Head Is - DuQuette, Lon Milo

Lucky You - How to Get Everything You Want and Create Your Ideal Life Using the Law of Attraction

Magical Secrets of the Psalms: Ancient Secrets On How To Achieve Your Wishes And Desires Using

The Psalms - Monroe, Shelia R.

Magic and the Law of Attraction: A Witch's Guide to the Magic of Intention, Raising Your Frequency,

and Building Your Reality - Chamberlain, Lisa

Magickal Cashbook: Attract Money Fast With Ancient Secrets And Modern Wealth Magick - Brand, Damon

Magickal Destiny: Experience The Power of Your Holy Guardian Angel - Brand, Damon

Mastering What You Practice: Learning to Control Your Emotions - Conte Ph.D., Christian

MASTERS OF THE SECRETS - The Science of Getting Rich and Master Key System Expanded

Michael: Communicating with the Archangel for Guidance & Protection (Angels Series, 1) - Webster, Richard

Mind is the Master: The Complete James Allen Treasury - Allen, James

My Life With The Spirits: The Adventures of a Modern Magician - DuQuette, Lon Milo

Never Argue with a Dead Person: True and Unbelievable Stories from the Other Side - John, Thomas

Old World Magick for the Modern World: Tips, Tricks, and Techniques to Balance, Empower, and Create a Life You Love - Negri, Patti

Oneness - Rasha

Opening to the Other Side: How to Become a Psychic or Medium - Craig Hamilton-Parker

Our Ultimate Reality, Life, the Universe and Destiny of Mankind - Cooper, Adrian P.

Pendulum Magic for Beginners: Tap Into Your Inner Wisdom - Webster, Richard

Practical Pendulum Book: With Instructions for Use and 38 Pendulum Charts - Jurriaanse, D.

Proof of Heaven: A Neurosurgeon's Journey into the Afterlife - Eben Alexander

Psychic Development for Beginners: An Easy Guide to Developing & Releasing Your Psychic

Psychic Perception: The Magic of Extrasensory Power (A miracles studies book) - Joseph Murphy

Psycho-Cybernetics, A New Way to Get More Living Out of Life - Maxwell Maltz

Raphael: Communicating with the Archangel for Healing & Creativity (Angels Series, 3) - Webster, Richard

Raziel's Paths of Power: Volume I: 72 Angels of the Name - Tempest, Jareth

Remote Viewing Secrets: A Handbook - McMoneagle, Joseph

Sacred Mirrors: The Visionary Art of Alex Grey - Grey, Alex

Scrying For Beginners (For Beginners (Llewellyn's)) - Donald Tyson

Secrets of Heaven (New Knowledge Library) - Summers, Marshall Vian

Secrets of Your Own Healing Power - Dr. Wayne W. Dyer

Sigils of Power and Transformation: 111 Magick Sigils to Change and Control Your Life - Blackthorne, Adam

Soul Healing Miracles: Ancient and New Sacred Wisdom, Knowledge, and Practical Techniques for Healing the Spiritual, Mental, Emotional, and Physical B - Sha, Zhi Gang

Success Through A Positive Mental Attitude - Napoleon Hill

Talk with Angels: How to Work with Angels of Light for Guidance, Comfort and Healing - Prophet, Elizabeth Clare

The Amazing Secrets of the Masters of the Far East - Robert Collier

The Angel of the Law of Attraction: 4 in 1- A Sacred Guide to Understanding and Manifest Money, Love, Success and Health in Our Lives-Bonus: the New Secrets to Winning the Lottery - Tohen, Isabel

The Angels of The Law of Attraction: Manifest Your Dreams With Divine Power - Manning, Rose

The Answer: Grow Any Business, Achieve Financial Freedom, and Live an Extraordinary Life - John Assaraf

The Art of Magick: The Mystery of Deep Magick & Divine Rituals (The Sacred Mystery) - Sarom, Gabriyell

The Art of True Healing: The Unlimited Power of Prayer and Visualization - Regardie, Israel

The Attractor Factor: 5 Easy Steps for Creating Wealth (or Anything Else) from the Inside Out - Joe Vitale (Author)

The Automatic Writing Experience (AWE): How to Turn Your Journaling into Channeling to Get

Unstuck, Find Direction, and Live Your Greatest Life! - Sandler, Michael

The Bhagavad Gita (Classic of Indian Spirituality) - Eknath Easwaran

The Biology of Belief: Unleashing the Power of Consciousness, Matter, & Miracles - Bruce H. Lipton Ph.D.

The Book of Magical Psalms - Part 1 - Swart, Jacobus G.

The Complete Encyclopedia of Angels: A Guide to 200 Celestial Beings to Help, Heal, and Assist

You in Everyday Life - Gregg, Susan

The Cosmic Energizer: Miracle Power of the Universe - Joseph Murphy

The Eye of the I: From Which Nothing Is Hidden - David R. Hawkins

The Four Agreements: A Practical Guide to Personal Freedom (A Toltec Wisdom Book) - Don Miguel Ruiz

The Game of Life And How To Play It - Florence Scovel Shinn

The Genie Within: Your Subconcious Mind--How It Works and How To Use It - Harry W Carpenter

The Golden Codes of Shamballa: Spiritual numbers to uplift humanity and multiply all the energies of

love, light, and happiness - Mylonas, Georgios

The Greater Words of Power: The Secret Calls of Archangel Magick - Brand, Damon

The Greatest Salesman in the World - Og Mandino

The Happy Medium: Life Lessons from the Other Side - Russo, Kim

The Healer's Manual: A Beginner's Guide to Energy Healing for Yourself and Others (Llewellyn's

Health & Healing) - Andrews, Ted

The Heart of the Buddha's Teaching - Thich Nhat Hanh

The Intention Experiment: Using Your Thoughts to Change Your Life and the World - Lynne McTaggart

The Kabbalah & Magic of Angels - González-Wippler, Migene

The Key: The Missing Secret for Attracting Anything You Want - Joe Vitale (Author)

The Last Law of Attraction Book You'll Ever Need To Read: The Missing Key To Finally Tapping Into

The Universe And Manifesting Your Desires - Kap, Andrew

The Law of Attraction: The Basics of the Teachings of Abraham - Hicks, Esther

The Life Magnet - Robert Collier

The Magic (The Secret) - Rhonda Byrne

The Magic of Believing - Claude M. Bristol

The Man Who Tapped the Secrets of the Universe - Glenn Clark

The Map: Finding the Magic and Meaning in the Story of Your Life - Colette Baron-Reid

The Map of Heaven: How Science, Religion, and Ordinary People Are Proving the Afterlife - Eben Alexander

The Mediums' Book - Kardec, Allan

The Miracle Club: How Thoughts Become Reality - Horowitz, Mitch

The New Science of Getting Rich - Wallace D. Wattles

The Power (The Secret) - Rhonda Byrne

The Power of Awareness - Goddard, Neville

The Power of Intention - Dr. Wayne W. Dyer

The Power of Your Mind: An Edgar Cayce Series Title - A R E Press

The Power of Your Subconscious Mind: Complete and Unabridged - Joseph Murphy

The Rider Tarot Deck Original Rider-Waite with Instruction Booklet by U.S. Games Systems

The Science of Mind - Earnest Holmes

The Secret of Light - Russell, Walter

The Secret of the Ages - Robert Collier

The Secret - Rhonda Byrne

The Silva Mind Control Method - Jose Silva

The Success System That Never Fails - William Clement Stone

The Wisdom of Wallace D. Wattles III - Including: The Science of Mind, The Road to Power AND

Your Invisible Power - Wattles, Wallace D.

Third Eye Awakening: The Ultimate Guide to Discovering New Perspectives, Increasing Awareness, Consciousness and Achieving Spiritual Enlightenment Through the Powerful Lens of the Third Eye -

Hughes, Ella

This Thing Called You - Ernest Holmes

Thoughts Are Things - Prentice Mulford

Three Magic Words: The Key to Power, Peace and Plenty - Andersen, U. S.

Transcending the Levels of Consciousness: The Stairway to Enlightenment - Hawkins M.D. Ph.D, David R.

Transcending the Levels of Consciousness - David R. Hawkins M.D. Ph.D.

Violet Flame to Heal Body, Mind and Soul (Pocket Guides to Practical Spirituality) - Prophet, Elizabeth Clare

Walking in the Garden of Souls: George Anderson's Advice from the Hereafter for Living in he Here

and Now - Anderson, George

Walking Through Anger: A New Design for Confronting Conflict in an Emotionally Charged World - Conte Ph.D., Christian

Wisdom from Your Spirit Guides: A Handbook to Contact Your Soul's Greatest Teachers Kindle Edition by James Van Praagh

Where Two Worlds Meet How to Develop Evidential Mediumship Janet Nohavec

Wishes Fulfilled: Mastering the Art of Manifesting - Dr. Wayne W. Dyer

Words of Power: Secret Magickal Sounds That Manifest Your Desires - Brand, Damon

You Are Psychic: Develop Your Natural Intuition Through Your Psychic Type - Dillard, Sherrie

You Are the Placebo: Making Your Mind Matter - Dispenza, Dr. Joe

Your Word Is Your Wand - Florence Scovel Shinn

ABOUT THE AUTHOR

Phyllis Okon is the CEO of an international ground transportation company she founded with her late husband in the 1970s.

She is the award-winning and best-selling author of over seventy books, as Carole P. Roman and Brit Lunden.

Never afraid to reinvent herself, she tackled mediumship during the pandemic. She studied with many of the top mediums in the country, including Seatbelt Psychic Thomas John, Kim Russo, and Joe Sheeil.

Phyllis has set up a practice as Lady Phyllis and is available for both in-person and Zoom sessions.

She lives near her children and grandchildren on Long Island, New York.

www.ingramcontent.com/pod-product-compliance
Lightning Source LLC
Chambersburg PA
CBHW052124110526
44592CB00013B/1737